ZY'KEE 123...

TEACH ME

ZY'KEE 123...

Cover design: Google and Cover Creator
Editor: T.R.A.C Publishing
Interior illustration: Google
Interior design: T.R.A.C Publishing
Bible Scriptures: New Living Translation
ISBN: 10: 0692357769
ISBN: 13: 978-0692357767
Library of Congress catalog card number:
Printed in the United States of America

DEDICATION

THIS BOOK IS DEDICATED TO MY GRANDSONS ZY'KEE PADILLA AND WILLIAM GARCIA, JR.

SIX YEARS AGO, I BECAME A GRANDMOTHER BY MY FIRST BORN DAUGHTER. GIVING ME A HANDSOME GRANDSON NAMED ZY'KEE. I MUST SAY HE IS A HANDFUL, BUT HE BRINGS ME JOY!

ZY'KEE IS MUCH LIKE MANY CHILDREN BUT THEN HE IS QUITE DIFFERENT. HE IS VERY MATURE FOR HIS AGE AND REQUIRES A LOT OF ATTENTION. ALSO, HE IS GROWING EVERY DAY AND LEARNING AS HE GROWS.

AS HIS GRANDMOTHER I DO NOT HAVE THE MONEY TO BUY HIM EVERYTHING HE WANTS. BUT THE ONE THING I HAVE MADE MYSELF ACCOUNTABLE FOR
IS TO TEACH HIM ABOUT THE LORD JESUS THE CHRIST!

I WANT HIM TO KNOW HOW TO RESPECT AND BE POLITE TO OTHERS AND THANK GOD FOR EVERY DAY THAT HE GIVES HIM LIFE.

ALSO, I WANT HIM TO APPRECIATE THE LITTLE THINGS HIS PARENTS ARE ABLE TO DO. EVEN IF THEY CANNOT DO IT ALL OR DO IT BIG!

TO TELL THE TRUTH, EVEN IF HE IS CAUGHT DOING WRONG, AND TAKE FULL RESPONSIBILITY!

WHEN HE ASKED ME TO WRITE HIM A BOOK, I WAS CHALLENGED BECAUSE I DO NOT WRITE CHILDREN BOOKS. BUT I COULD NOT SAY NO TO MY GRANDSON. SO… "ZY'KEE PADILLA HERE'S TO YOU AND MANY OF YOUR FRIENDS AND HOPEFULLY CHILDREN ALL AROUND THE WORLD!"

I HOPE YOU ENJOY IT ZY'MAN BABY!!!

WILLIAM GARCIA, JR. I KNOW THIS BOOK WILL SOON BE IN YOUR HANDS AND YOU WILL READ EVERY WORD TO YOUR GAGA…

"YOU ARE MORE THAN FOUR HANDFULS SO I AM NOT SURE WHAT YOUR PARENTS ARE GOING TO WITH YOU - CURIOUS WILL!"

I PRAY THAT THE SEEDS SOWN THROUGH THIS BOOK, AND THE BOOKS TO COME, TEACHES THE CHILDREN ON THEIR LEVEL OF UNDERSTANDING AND STRETCHES THEM TO LEARN MORE. GOD BLESS YOU!

ACKNOWLEDGEMENTS

GIVING THANKS TO MY DAUGHTERS, SHUKRIYYAH AND SHANICE EDNESS FOR TWO HANDSOME GRANDSONS.

ALSO, THANKS TO THEIR SONS FATHERS BRIAN PADILLA AND WILLIAM GRACIA, SR.

IT REALLY TAKES TWO PARENTS TO RAISE A CHILD THAT WILL GROW UP BALANCED IN EVERY AREA OF THEIR LIVES.

IT TAKES TWO PARENTS TO COMMUNICATE EFFECTIVELY AND TO BE ACTIVE IN THEIR EVERY DAY LIVES, IN ORDER TO RAISE THEM TO BE A BLESSING TO THE WORLD AND AN HONOR TO THEIR PARENTS.

YOUR CHILDREN ARE YOUR DONATION TO THE WORLD!

THEY WILL IMITATE ONLY WHAT THEY SEE YOU DO AND HEAR YOU SAY!

BE CAREFUL HOW YOU TREAT ONE ANOTHER AND HOW YOU TREAT THEM, BECAUSE SOON THEY WILL TREAT YOU AND OTHERS THE SAME.

DO NOT RAISE YOUR CHILDREN EXACTLY THE SAME WAY YOU WERE RAISED. DO NOT RAISE THEM COMPLETELY DIFFERENT FROM THE WAY YOU WERE RAISED.

DO NOT GIVE THEM WHAT YOU WANTED BECAUSE YOUR PARENTS WEREN'T ABLE TO GIVE IT YOU. DO NOT ALLOW THEM TO DO WHAT YOU WEREN'T ABLE TO DO.

IN OTHER WORDS, I AM SAYING THIS IS A NEW TIME AND A NEW GENERATION. THE BEST WAY OF RAISING YOUR CHILDREN IS TO RAISE THEM WITH THE FEAR OF GOD!

TAKE SOME OF THE GOOD TEACHINGS FROM YOUR PARENTS AND WHAT WAS BAD, DO NOT USE.

GIVE THEM WHAT YOU CAN, BUT THE BEST GIFT TO GIVE ANY CHILD IS THE LOVE OF JESUS!

INTRODUCE THEM TO JESUS AND ALLOW THEM TO SEE YOUR RELATIONSHIP WITH CHRIST. WITH THE HOPES THEY WILL DESIRE TO HAVE A RELATIONSHIP WITH HIM AS WELL.

MAY GOD BLESS EVERY PARENT THAT SOWS THIS SEED INTO THEIR CHILDREN LIVES. BLESSINGS…

INTRODUCTION

THIS BOOK IS DESIGNED TO TEACH OUR CHILDREN, OUR FUTURE, THE LOVE AND FEAR OF GOD THROUGH SCRIPTURES.

ALSO, A TOOL USED TO TEACH THEM THEIR NUMBERS IN ENGLISH AND SPANISH, COLORS, DAYS OF THE WEEK, MONTHS OF THE YEAR, AND HOW TO STAY SAFE AND OUT OF HARMS WAY.

TEACHING THEM TO HONOR THEIR PARENTS, RESPECT ALL PEOPLE, TELL THE TRUTH, AND BE RESPONSIBLE CHILDREN; SO THEY CAN GROW TO BE RESPONSIBLE MATURE ADULTS.

I PRAY THIS BOOK REACHES THE SHELVES IN MANY HOMES, SCHOOLS, AND CHURCH LIBRARIES.

WE MUST TRAIN UP OUR CHILDREN IN THE WAY THEY SHALL GO, SO WHEN THEY GROW OLDER THEY WILL NOT DEPART FROM IT. AMEN.

THIS IS MY SEED AND AS THEY READ; THE SEED WILL BE PLANTED, WATERED, AND GOD WILL BRING THE INCREASE
IN JESUS' NAME AMEN!

I PRAY THAT EVERY WORD TAKE ROOT AND
BEAR MUCH FRUIT IN THE LIVES OF OUR
CHILDREN
IN JESUS' NAME AMEN…

ZY'KEE 123...
TEACH ME

1

UNO

ONE

ONE GOD,
ONE HOLY SPIRIT
ONE SON; JESUS THE CHRIST

"YOU MUST NOT HAVE ANY OTHER
GOD BUT ME."
EXODUS 20:3

DO NOT PUT YOUR TOYS, NICE
CLOTHES, OR ANYTHING ELSE
BEFORE GOD!

2

DOS

TWO

A FATHER + A MOTHER = TWO PARENTS

"HONOR YOUR FATHER & YOUR MOTHER"
EPHESIANS 6:12

A FATHER KEEPS PEOPLE FROM HURTING YOU. HE BUYS YOU CLOTHES, CELLULAR PHONES, AND GAMES.
A MOTHER COOKS FOR YOU, WASH YOUR CLOTHES, SHAMPOO YOUR HAIR, BATHES YOU, IRON YOUR CLOTHES, ROCKS YOU ASLEEP, READS TO YOU, HELPS YOU WITH YOUR HOMEWORK, AND KISSES YOU AT BEDTIME.
YOU NEED THEM BOTH & THEY BOTH LOVE YOU!

3

TRES

THREE

THREE WORD PHRASES YOU
SHOULD KNOW AND USE.

THANK YOU…
YOU'RE WELCOME …
I APOLOGIZE …

Please and thank you

are still magic words!

{No matter how old you are!}

OR HOW YOUNG YOU ARE!

4

CUATRO

FOUR

LOVE THY NEIGHBOR AS YOURSELF
MARK 12:31

TO OBEY IS BETTER THAN GIVING
1 SAMUEL 15:22

PRAY WITHOUT STOPPING
1 THESSALONIANS 5:16

KIND WORDS TURN AWAY ANGER
PROVERBS 15:1

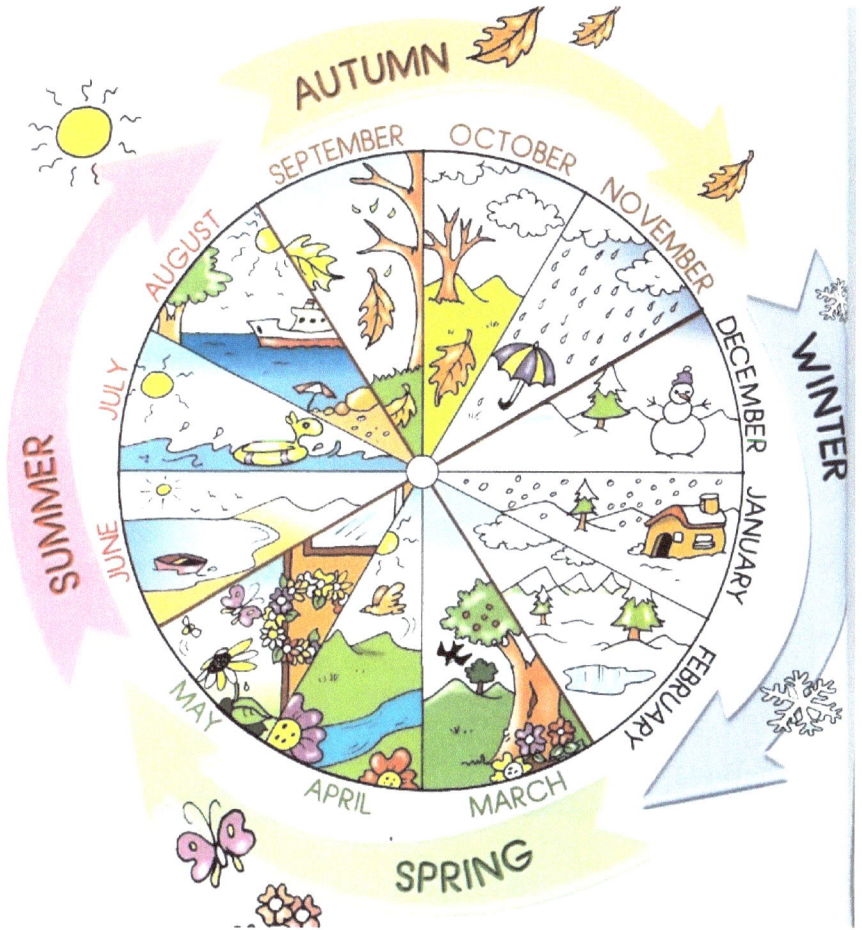

SEASONS CHANGES FOUR TIMES A YEAR.

5

CINCO

FIVE

THE FIVE SENSES

SEE
FEEL
HEAR
TASTE
SMELL

2 CORINTHIANS 2:15
OUR LIVES ARE LIKE A CHRIST-LIKE
FRAGRANCE RISING UP TO GOD.

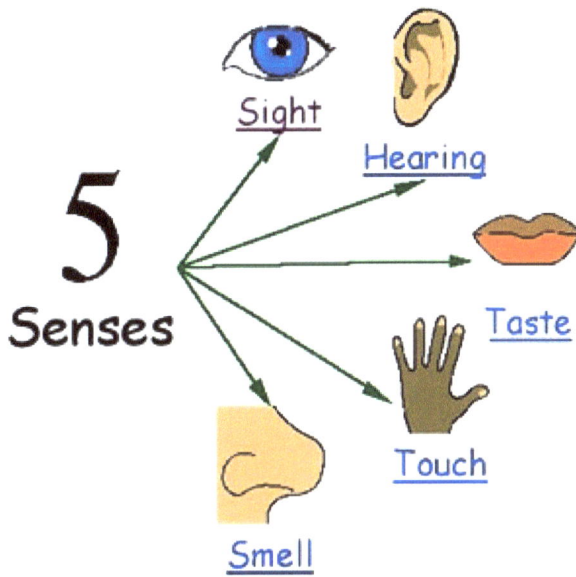

5 Senses — Sight, Hearing, Taste, Touch, Smell

KEEP YOUR EYES ON JESUS!

GOD'S CHILDREN KNOW HIS VOICE AND THEY DO NOT GO WITH STRANGERS!

TASTE AND SEE THAT THE LORD IS GOOD!

EVERYTHING YOU TOUCH WILL BE BLESSED!

6

SEIS

SIX

THERE ARE SIX IMPORTANT
QUESTIONS THAT YOU MUST ASK
YOURSELF AND OTHERS BEFORE
MAKING A DECISION.

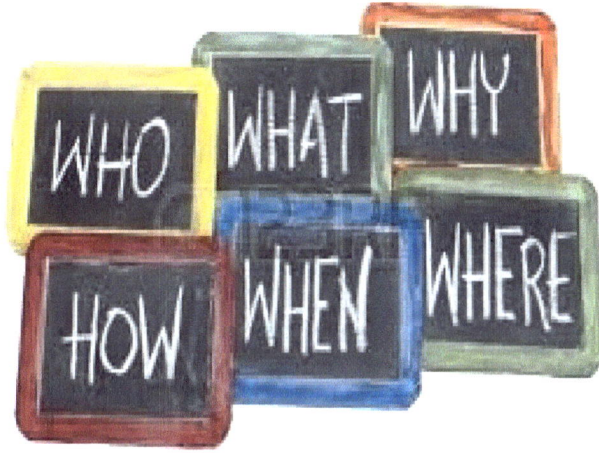

WHO IS A PERSON?

WHAT IS A THING?

WHY IS THE REASON?

HOW IS INSTRUCTIONS OR
DIRECTIONS?

WHEN IS A DATE AND TIME?

WHERE IS A PLACE?

7

SIETE

SEVEN

THERE ARE SEVEN DAYS IN A WEEK

YOU ATTEND CHURCH ON SUNDAYS

SCHOOL MONDAY THROUGH
FRIDAY

SATURDAYS, LET'S PLAY!!

DAYS OF THE WEEK

Sunday
Monday
Tuesday
Wednesday
Thursday
Friday
Saturday

ALWAYS KEEP THE SABBATH DAY HOLY!

8

OCHO

EIGHT

NUMBER EIGHT MEANS NEW
BEGINNINGS...

ALL THINGS ARE MADE BRAND
NEW...

YOU WILL MEET

NEW FRIENDS
NEW TEACHERS
GO TO NEW SCHOOLS
MOVE TO NEW NEIGHBORHOODS
HAVE NEW EXPERIENCES
NEW CREATIVITY
NEW WAY OF THINKING
&
A HAPPY NEW YEAR!

9

NUEVE

NINE

THERE ARE NINE IMPORTANT
PEOPLE TO YOU BESIDES GOD AND
YOURSELF!

APPRECIATE ALL OF THEM!

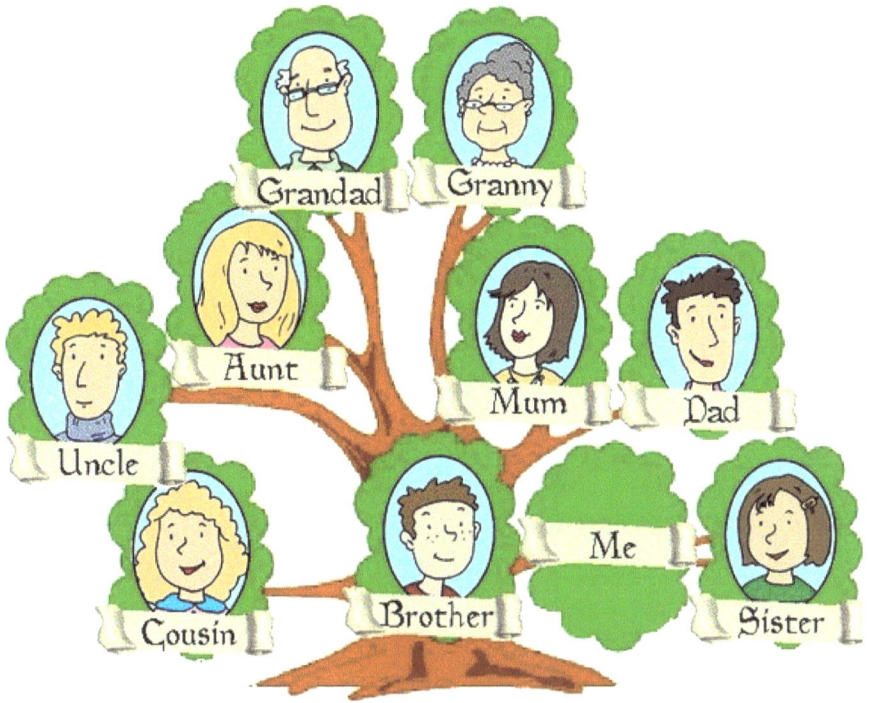

GOD FIRST
THEN YOU
NEXT ARE YOUR PARENTS

THEY WILL ALL HAVE A SPECIAL
PLACE IN YOUR HEART AND YOU
WILL HAVE ONE IN THEIRS.

10
DIEZ
TEN

YOU SHALL NOT:
STEAL, DO DRUGS, DRINK BEER,
SMOKE CIGARETTES OR WEED,
BULLY OTHERS, LIE TO OR ON
OTHERS,
CURSE, HATE, MISTREAT, OR
DISRESPECT ANYONE!

God's BIG 10

1. Love God more than you Love anything else.

2. Don't make anything in your life more important than God.

3. Always say God's name with Love and Respect.

4. Honor the Lord by resting on the seventh day of the week.

5. Love and Respect your Mom and Dad.

6. Never hurt anyone.

7. Always be faithful to your husband or wife.

8. Don't take anything that isn't yours.

9. Always tell the truth.

10. Be happy with what you have. Do not wish for other people's things.

ALWAYS KEEP GOD'S COMMANDMENTS!

11

ONCE ELEVEN

ELEVEN GOLDEN RULES!

PAY CLOSE ATTENTION BECAUSE
THEY WILL KEEP YOU SAFE AND
OUT OF TROUBLE!

1. DO NOT TALK TO STRANGERS!
2. DO NOT LEAVE YOUR SCHOOL WITH STRANGERS!
3. DO NOT GET IN THE CAR WITH STRANGERS!
4. DO NOT OPEN YOUR DOOR FOR ANYONE!
5. DO NOT ANSWER THE PHONE!
6. DO NOT GO INTO OTHER PEOPLE'S HOUSES!
7. DO NOT LET ANYONE TOUCH YOU INAPPROPRIATELY!
8. DO NOT GIVE ANYONE YOUR ADDRESS!
9. DO NOT GIVE ANYONE YOUR PHONE NUMBER!
10. DO NOT LET PEOPLE KISS YOU IN THE MOUTH!
11. DO NOT DRINK OR EAT AFTER OTHERS!

ALWAYS LET SOMEONE KNOW WHEN YOU ARE UNCOMFORTABLE!

12

DOCE

TWELVE

THERE ARE SOME VERY IMPORTANT
DATES YOU MUST REMEMBER
THROUGHOUT THE TWELVE
MONTHS!

LET'S FIRST START WITH THE BIRTH
OF JESUS
ON CHRISTMAS, DECEMBER 25TH

EASTER, THE DAY HE GOT UP AND
OUT OF THE GRAVE!

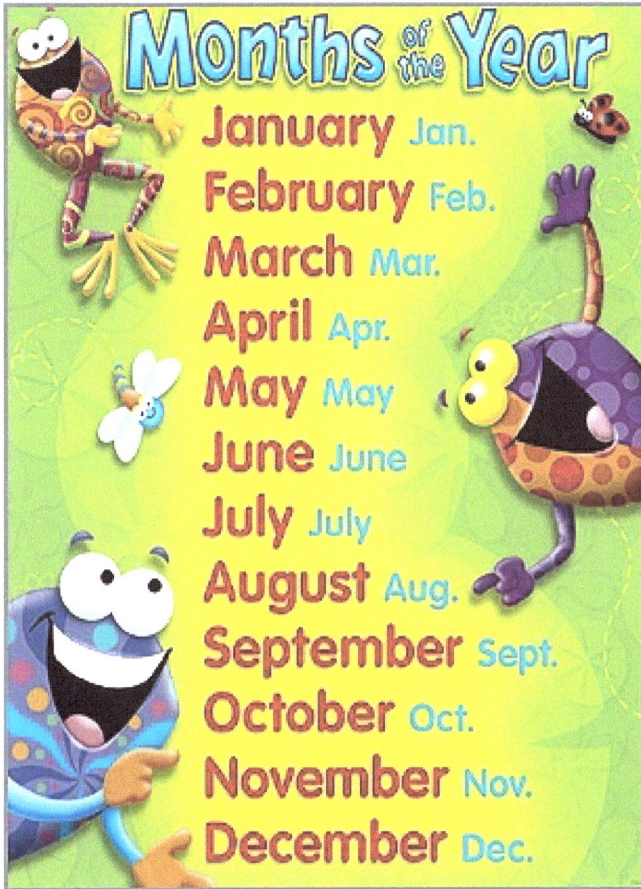
Months of the Year

January Jan.
February Feb.
March Mar.
April Apr.
May May
June June
July July
August Aug.
September Sept.
October Oct.
November Nov.
December Dec.

NEVER FORGET YOUR MOTHER'S BIRTHDAY!

DID I MENTION YOUR FATHER'S BIRTHDAY?

THEY WILL NEVER FORGET YOURS!

ALWAYS REMEMBER

WRONG is **WRONG**, even if *everyone* is doing it.

RIGHT is **RIGHT**, even if *no one* is doing it.

LOVE,
GRANDMA

GRANDSON NEVER GO TO
BED WITHOUT SAYING
GOODNIGHT
AND NEVER WAKE UP
WITHOUT SAYING
GOOD MORNING!

TOMORROW IS PROMISED
BUT YOU ARE NOT
PROMISED TO SEE
TOMORROW.
SO ALWAYS
THANK GOD
FOR
TODAY!

GOD BLESS YOU…

ABOUT THE AUTHOR

SHAKISHA EDNESS IS THE OLDEST OF THREE CHILDREN, MOTHER OF THREE, AND GRANDMOTHER OF TWO GRANDSONS.

SHE IS A WRITER, MENTOR, MOTIVATIONAL SPEAKER, TEACHER, AND EVANGELIST FOR CHRIST.

SHE SPEAKS THE TRUTH, CHANGES PERCEPTION, AND GAINS LIVES TO CHRIST.

SHE WAS BORN AND PARTIALLY RAISED IN NEWARK, NEW JERSEY. SHE MOVED TO AUSTELL, GEORGIA AT AGE TEN, WHERE SHE STILL RESIDES.

SHE HAS MENTORED IN LOCAL SCHOOLS IN HER AREA.

SHE IS AN ACTIVE MEMBER OF WORD OF FAITH FAMILY WORSHIP CATHEDRAL WHERE BISHOP DALE C. BRONNER IS THE SHEPHERD IN CHARGE.

SHE SITS UNDER GREAT LEADERSHIP THAT SHE MAY LEAD GREATLY!
BLESSINGS…

CHILDREN BOOKS BY
AUTHOR
SHAKISHA EDNESS

ZY'KEE 123…
ZY'KEE ABC…

www.ingramcontent.com/pod-product-compliance
Lightning Source LLC
Chambersburg PA
CBHW041808040426
42449CB00001B/10